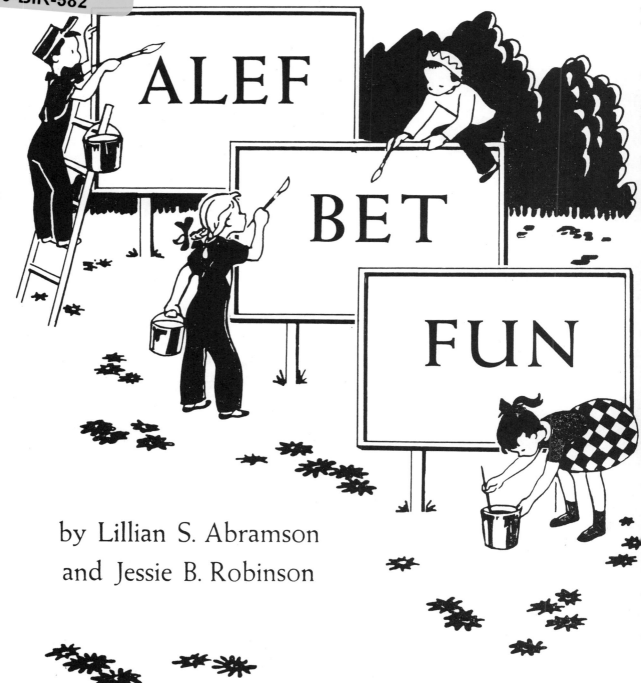

ALEF BET FUN

by Lillian S. Abramson
and Jessie B. Robinson

BLOCH PUBLISHING COMPANY, NEW YORK

Published by Bloch Publishing Company, Inc.
New York

Library of Congress Cataloging-in-Publication Data

Abramson, Lillian S.
    Alef bet fun / by Lillian S. Abramson, Jessie B. Robinson
       p.   cm.
    Summary: A guide, with exercises and games, for learning the names
and sequence of the letters of the Hebrew alphabet.
    ISBN 0-8197-0621-3
    1. Hebrew language--Alphabet--Juvenile literature.   [1. Hebrew
language--Alphabet.   2. Alphabet.]   I. Robinson, Jessie.
II. Title.
PJ4589.A18   1996
[E]--dc20   96-22922
                                              CIP
                                                 AC

PRINTED IN THE UNITED STATES OF AMERICA

Introduction

THIS BOOK has two specific aims: to help children learn the **names** of the letter in the Hebrew alphabet and to help them learn the **sequence** of those letters.

There is much good educational material in the field for the teaching of reading and writing of Hebrew. Children have been attaining these 2 r's successfully. It has been noted, however, that many students, even those in higher grades, can not identify by name many of the members of the Alef Bet. Few, indeed, know the entire Hebrew alphabet from beginning to end.

This book uses many play devices as drills, all with the attempt to accomplish its two main objectives. It is hoped that the children using this book of ALEF BET FUN will derive great pleasure from the games, dot pictures, mazes, etc. found herein and, at the same time, have their knowledge of the Hebrew alphabet greatly reinforced.

Children can use this book on their own, without the active supervision of an instructor.

L.S.A.

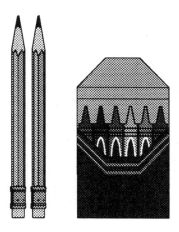

Dear Children,

Here is your very own book about the Alef Bet. It will give you many hours of play with the Hebrew letters.

You will do coloring and connect dot-to-dot pictures. You will find games to play with your friends and other fun activities to enjoy.

While you are playing, you are learning. Soon you will know the names of all the letters in the Alef Bet from first to last. You will know them in the right order from beginning to end.

Get your pencil and crayons ready, get set and get smart!

Have fun with your book!

L.S.A.

Alef

Print an alef in each balloon.

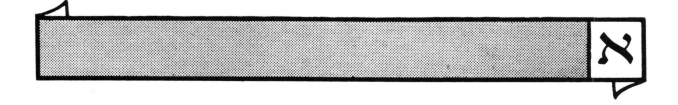

ב
Bet

Draw a line from א (alef) to ב (bet).

Print bet in this box.

Color alef blue.
Color bet red.

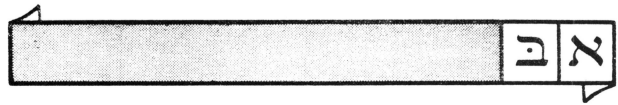

גּ

Gimel

Print gimel
in this box.

Connect the dots from א (alef) to בּ (bet) and from בּ (bet) to ג (gimel).

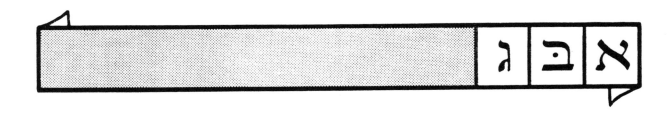

Color all spaces marked alef, red.
Color all spaces marked bet , yellow.
Color all spaces marked gimel, green.

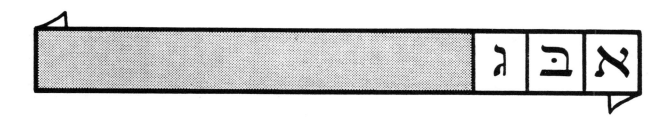

ד

Dalet

Print dalet
in the box.

Connect all the dots in the proper order (alef, bet, gimel, dalet).

Print the Hebrew letters in the balloons.

ד ג ב א

הַ

Hai

Print hai
in the box.

Connect all the dots in proper order from אָ (alef) to הַ (hai).

ו

Vov

Print vov
in the box.

Connect all the dots in proper order from **א** (alef) to **ו** (vov).

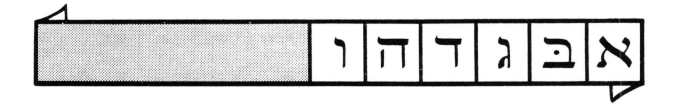

ו ה ד ג ב א

alef

gimel

bet

vov

hai

dalet

Print the Hebrew letters in the boxes.

אבגדהו

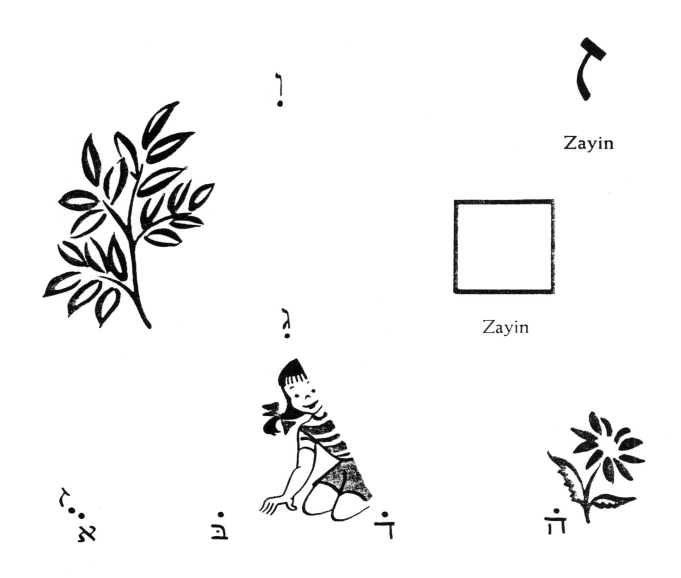

Zayin

Zayin

Connect all the dots in proper order from א (alef) to ז (zayin).

חֵ

Chet

Chet

Connect all the dots in proper order from א (alef) to ח (chet).

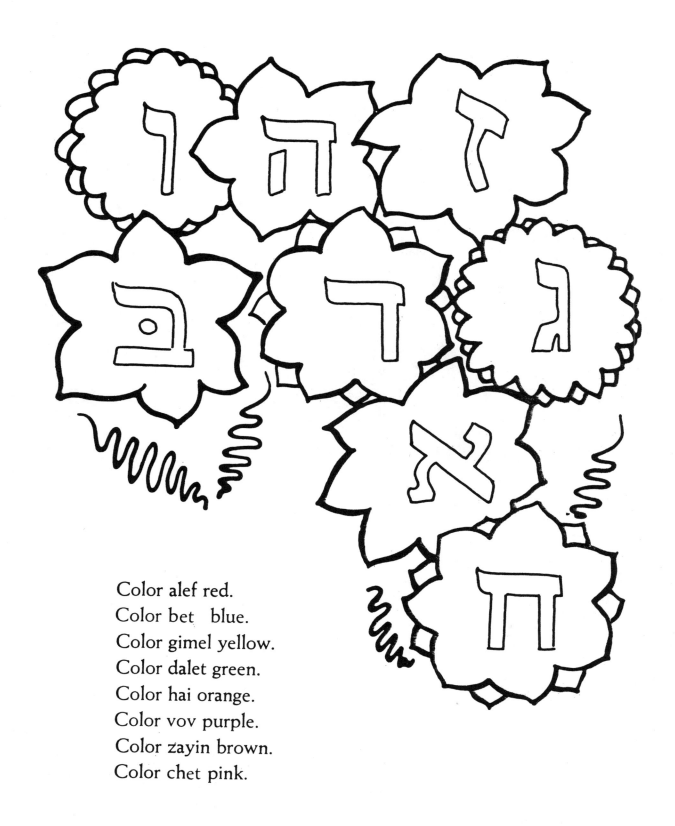

Color alef red.
Color bet blue.
Color gimel yellow.
Color dalet green.
Color hai orange.
Color vov purple.
Color zayin brown.
Color chet pink.

ט

Tet

Tet

Connect the dots in proper order from א (alef) to ט (tet).

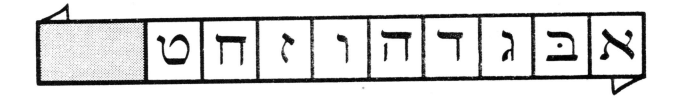

י

Yud

Yud

Connect the dots in proper order from **א** (alef) to **י** (yud).

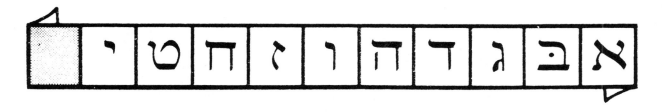

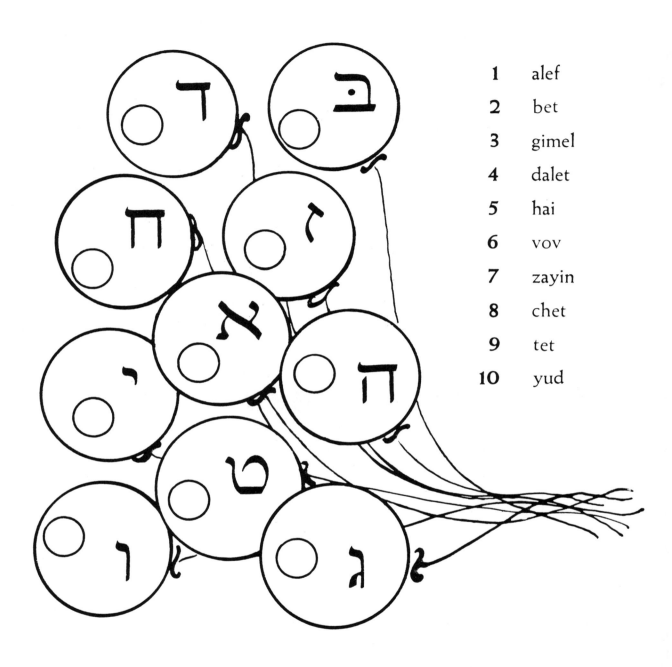

1   alef
2   bet
3   gimel
4   dalet
5   hai
6   vov
7   zayin
8   chet
9   tet
10 yud

Match the letters with their names.

Write the correct number in the circle next to each letter.

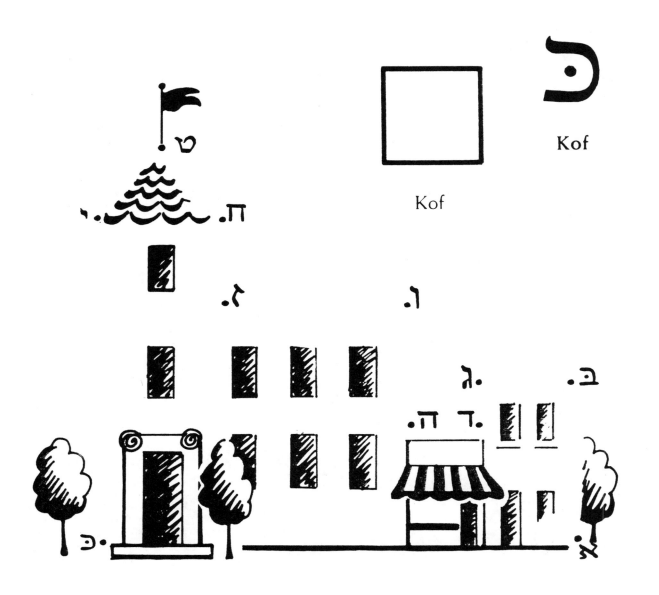

כ

Kof

Kof

Connect the dots in proper order from א (alef) to כ (kof).

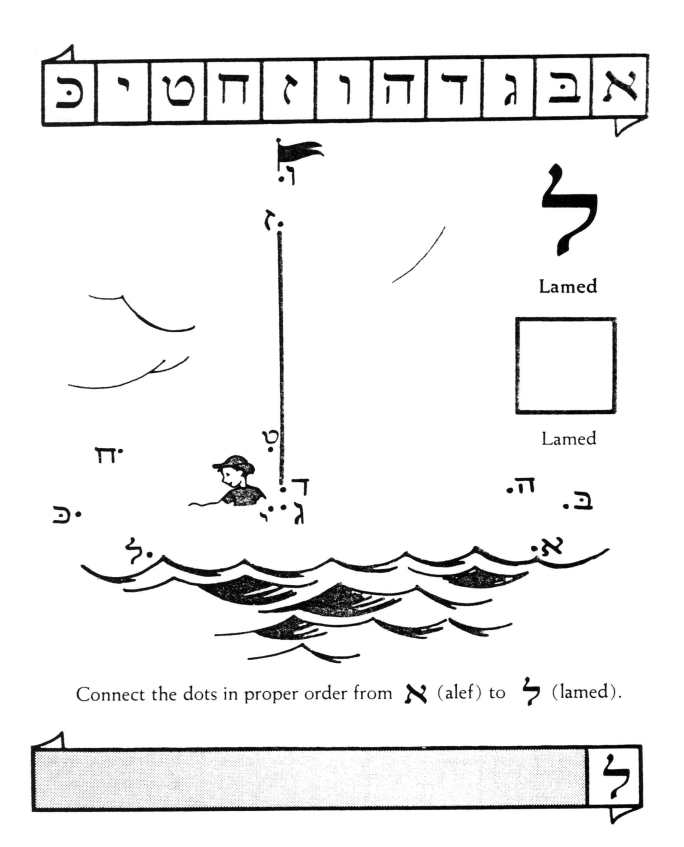

אבגדהוזחטיכ

ל

Lamed

Lamed

Connect the dots in proper order from א (alef) to ל (lamed).

ל

alef

bet

gimel

dalet

hai

vov

zayin

chet

tet

yud

kof

lamed

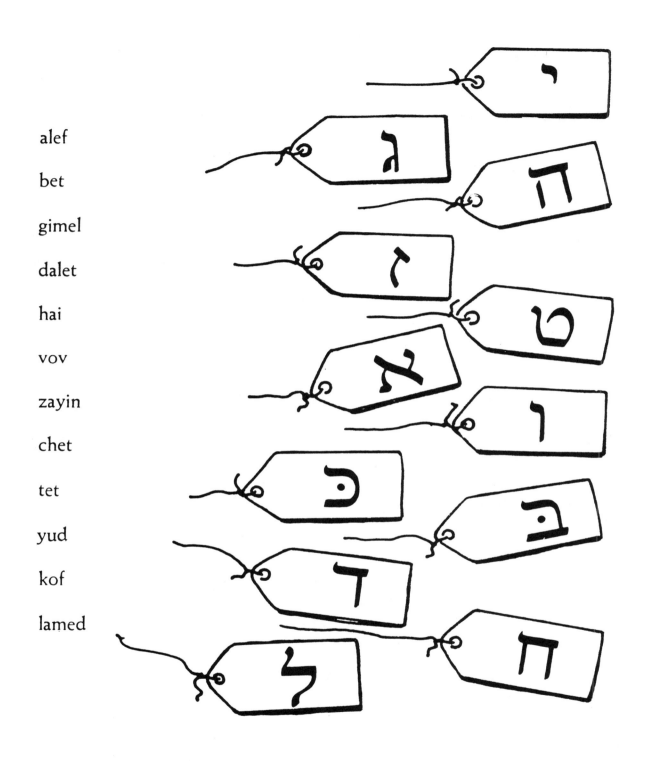

Draw a line from the name of the letter to the letter.

25

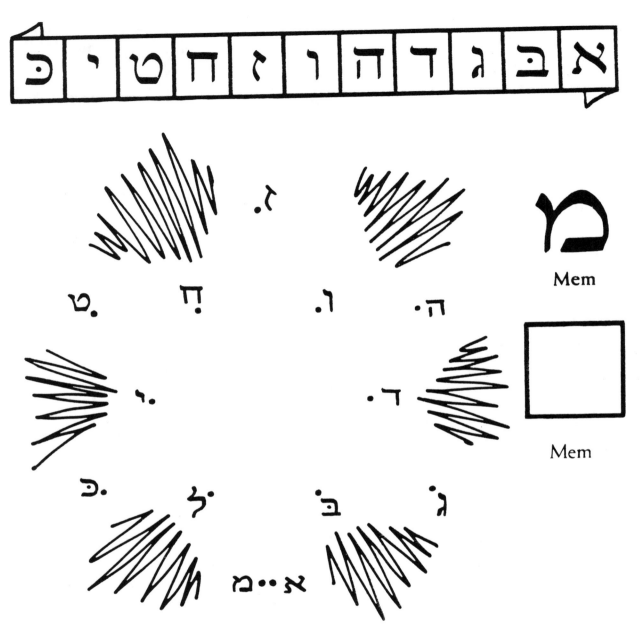

Connect the dots in proper order from א (alef) to מ (mem).

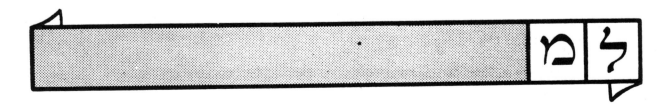

נ

Nun

Nun

Connect the dots in proper order from **א** (alef) to **נ** (nun).

ל מ נ

Color these letters and write the name of each letter under its window.

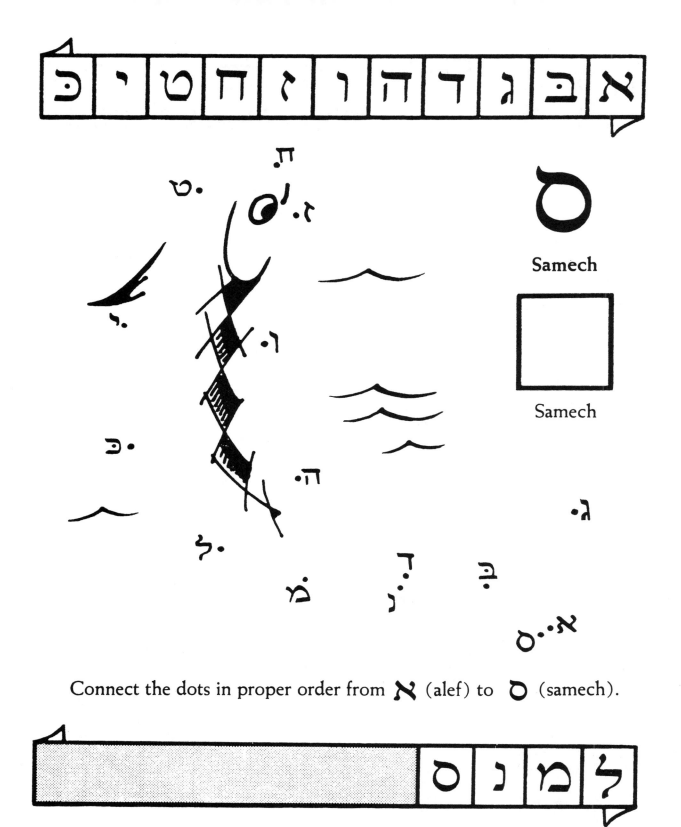

כ | י | ט | ח | ז | ו | ה | ד | ג | ב | א

ס

Samech

Samech

Connect the dots in proper order from א (alef) to ס (samech).

ל | מ | נ | ס

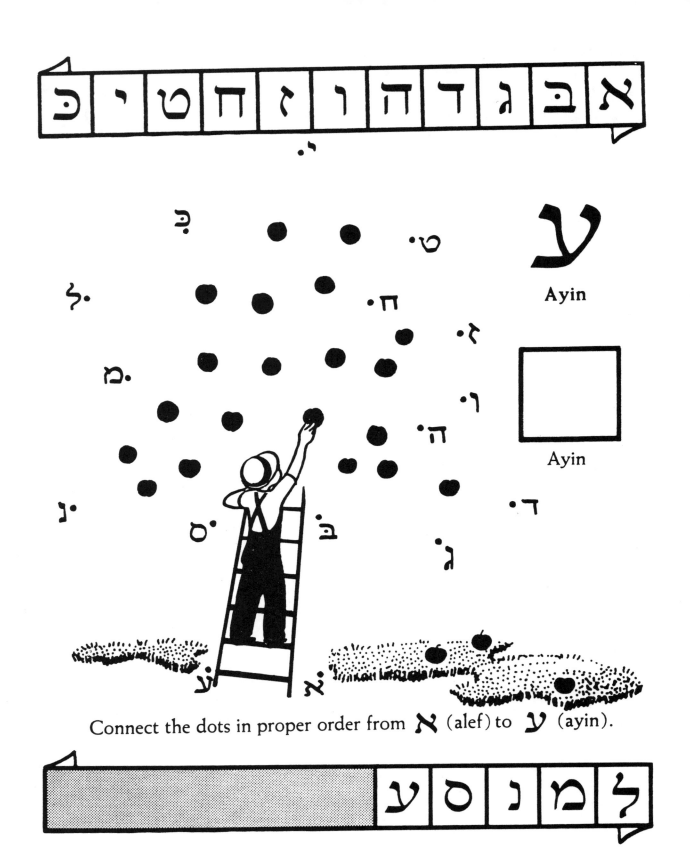

Connect the dots in proper order from א (alef) to ע (ayin).

Ayin

Ayin

Print the letters from alef to ayin in their correct order on the cards the children are carrying. Write the name of the letter underneath.

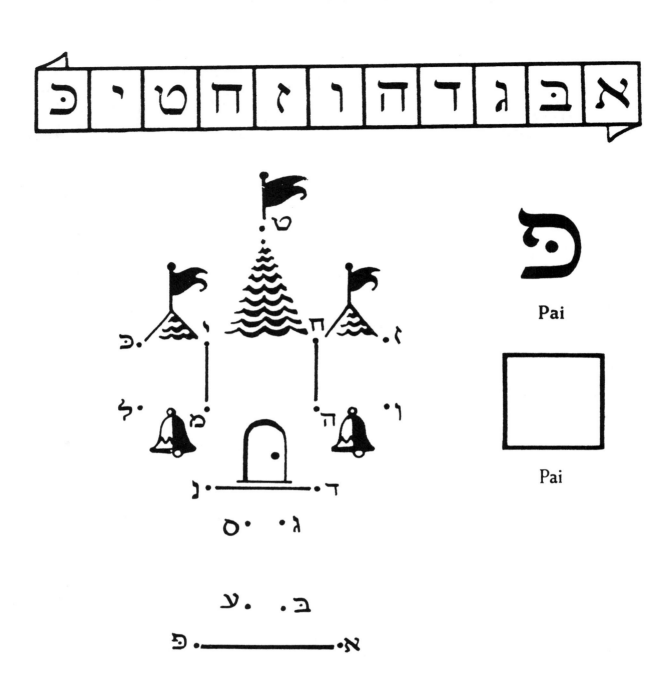

פ

Pai

Pai

Connect the dots in proper order from א (alef) to פ (pai).

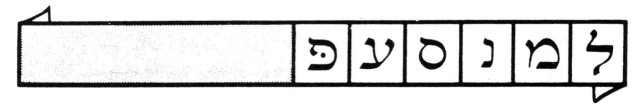

ל מ נ ס ע פ

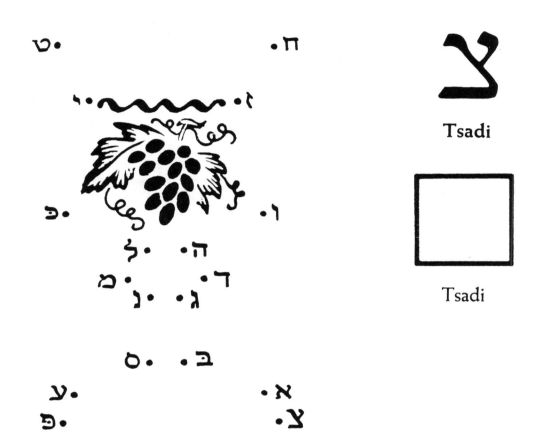

צ

Tsadi

Tsadi

Connect the dots in proper order from **א** (alef) to **צ** (tsadi).

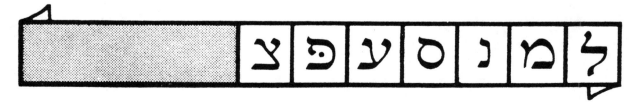

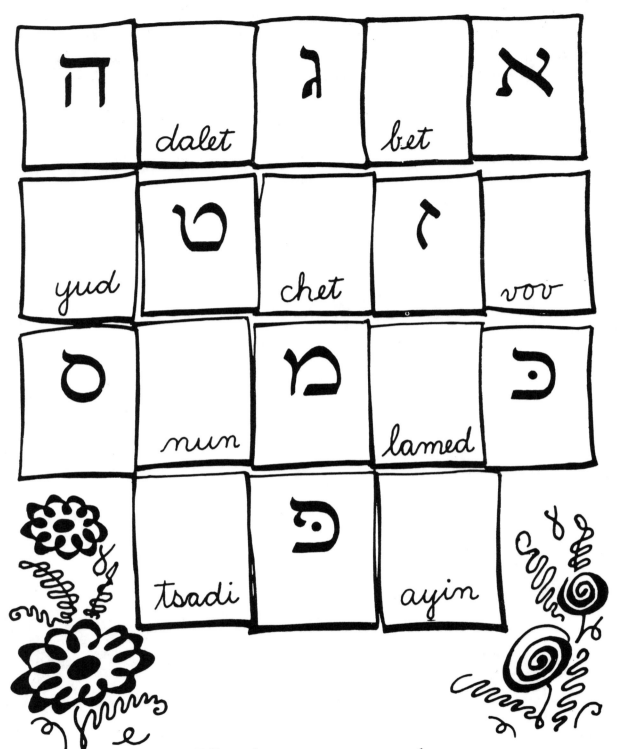

ה	_dalet_	ג	_bet_	א
yud	ט	_chet_	י	_vov_
ס	_nun_	מ	_lamed_	כ
tsadi	צ	_ayin_		

Fill in the missing names or letters.

כ	י	ט	ח	ז	ו	ה	ד	ג	ב	א

ק

Koof

Koof

Connect the dots in proper order from א (alef) to ק (koof).

	ק	צ	פ	ע	ס	נ	מ	ל

35

כ י ט ח ז ו ה ד ג ב א

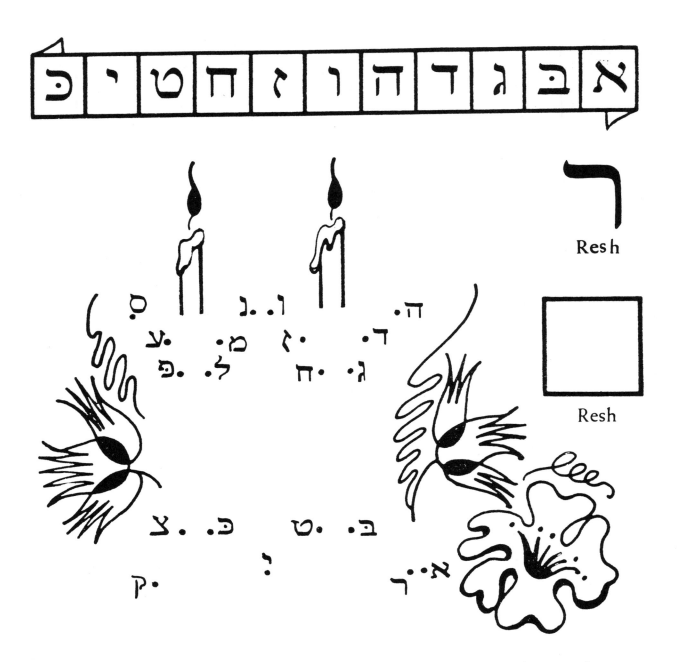

ר

Resh

Resh

Connect the dots in proper order from א (alef) to ר (resh).

ל מ נ ס ע פ צ ק ר

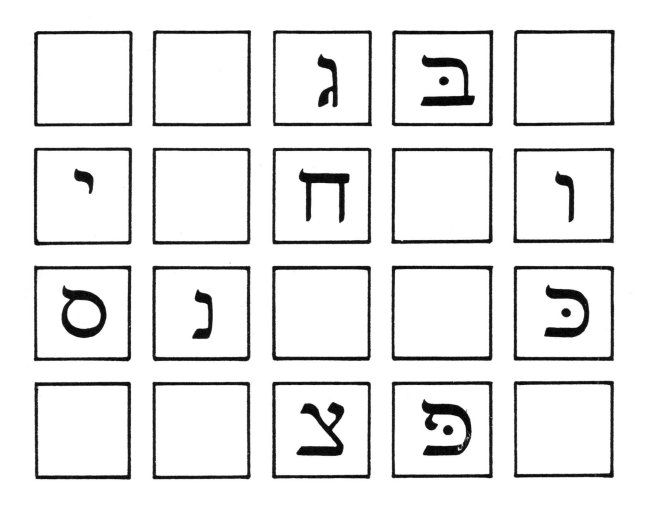

The letters below have fallen out of their boxes.

Print them where they belong.

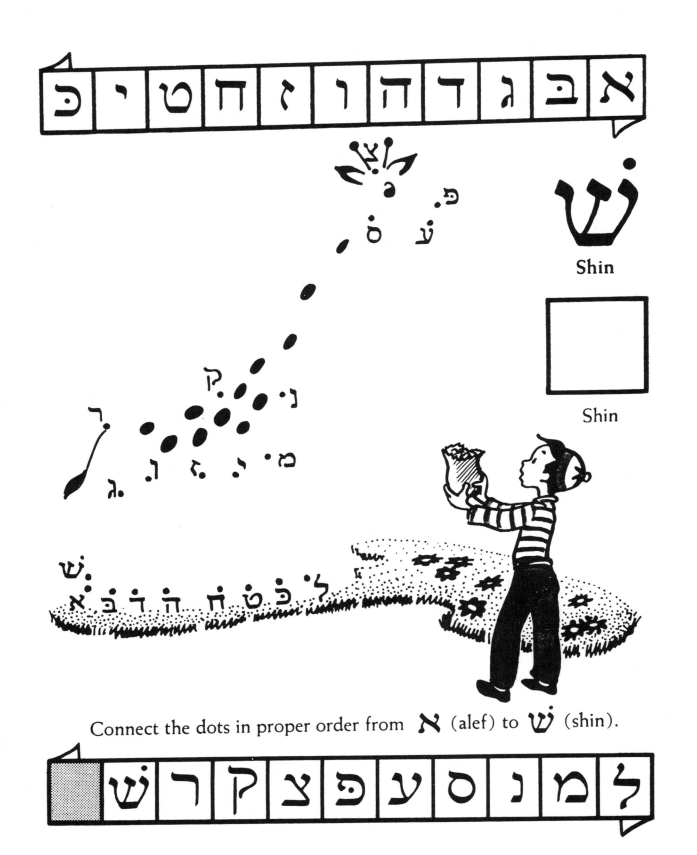

א ב ג ד ה ו ז ח ט י כ

שׁ

Shin

Shin

Connect the dots in proper order from א (alef) to שׁ (shin).

ל מ נ ס ע פ צ ק ר שׁ

א ב ג ד ה ו ז ח ט י כ

תּ

Tov

Tov

Connect the dots in proper order from א (alef) to תּ (tov).

ל מ נ ס ע פ צ ק ר שׁ תּ

39

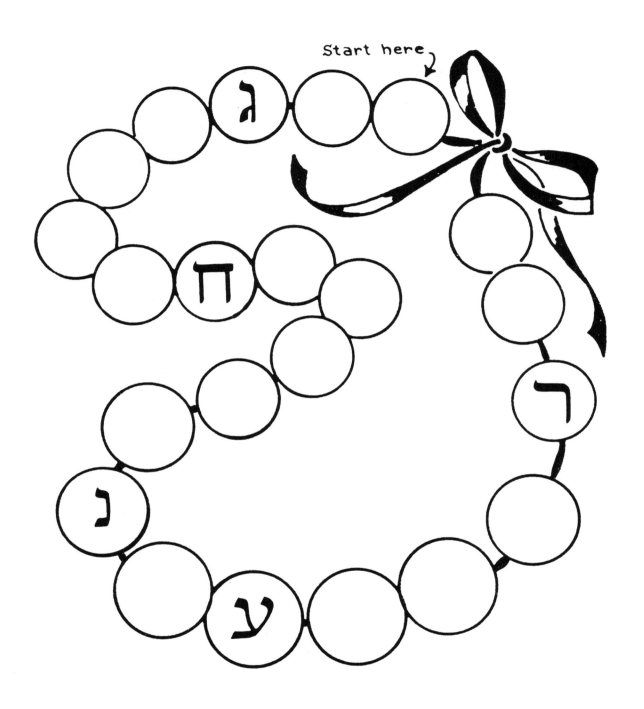

Start here

Fill in the missing letters of the Alef Bet.

ט	ח	ג	ז	ר	מ	כ	א	ל
ק	ד	שׁ	ת	לִ	ר	ע	ק
ר	י	תֵ	ק	י	שׁ	ט	שׁ
שׁ	נ	ק	ב	שׁ	ס	ת	ל	ר
ת	ר	שׁ	ת	ר	ת	ק	שׁ	ת
ס	ו	א	נ	ק	צ	מ	ח
ב	צ	כ	ד	ה	ת	כ	פ	ס
ל	ר	ת	ק	שׁ	ר	ת	ק	א

Color **only** the squares with the letters koof, resh, shin and tov.

41

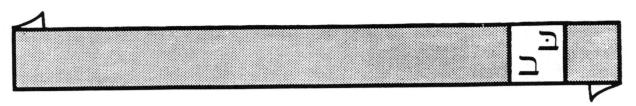

Some letters in the Alef Bet that have dots change when the dots are taken away.

בּ bet   without the dot is   ב vet

Vet

Vet

Bet

Color vet red.   Color bet yellow.

כ kof without the dot is כ chof.

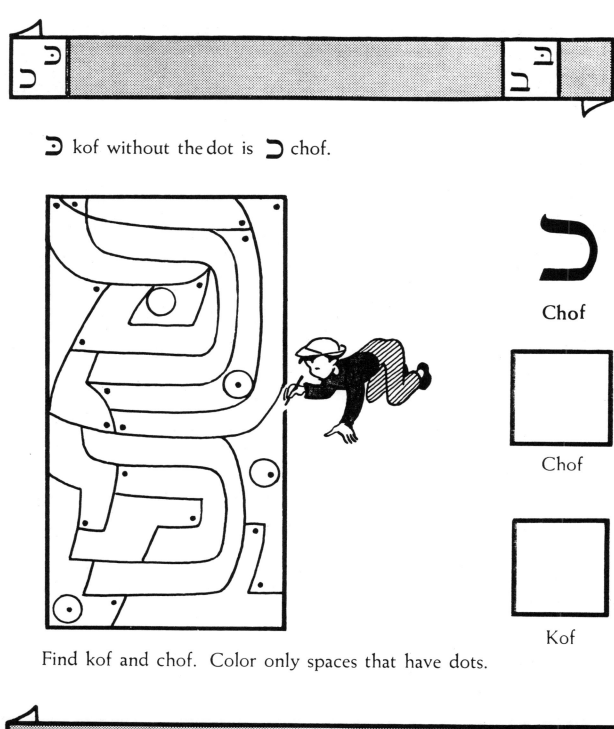

Chof

Chof

Kof

Find kof and chof. Color only spaces that have dots.

כ pai without the dot is כ fai.

Fai

Find fai.

Color **only** spaces that have dots.

Fai

Pai

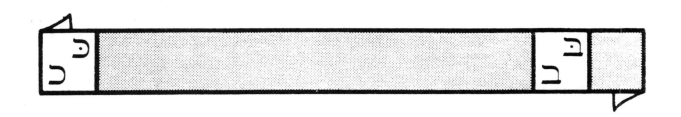

But  tov without the dot is still ת tov.

Color tov.

ת

Tov

Tov

Tov

45

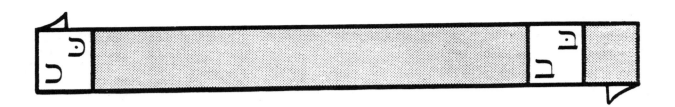

ש shin with its dot on the other side is שׂ sin.

שׂ
Sin

Find sin.

Color **only** spaces that have dots.

Sin

Shin

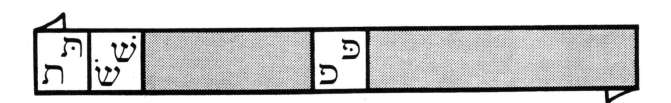

Color bet   red.   Color vet   pink.
Color kof yellow.   Color chof orange.
Color pai blue.   Color fai purple.
Color tov green.   Color tov brown.
Color shin orange.   Color sin blue.

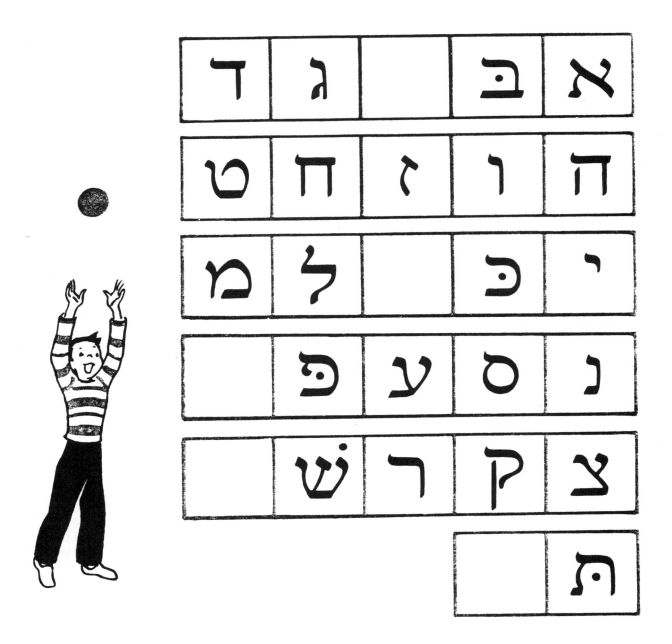

Put letters without dots after letters with dots in the Alef Bet.

שׁ is after שׂ

Print ב כ ת פ and שׁ where they belong.

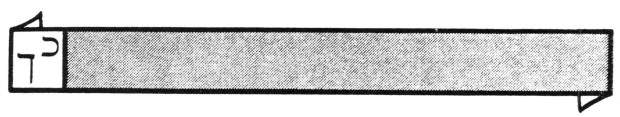

There are 5 letters in the Alef Bet that look different when they are at the end of a word.

כ chof at the end of a word looks like this:

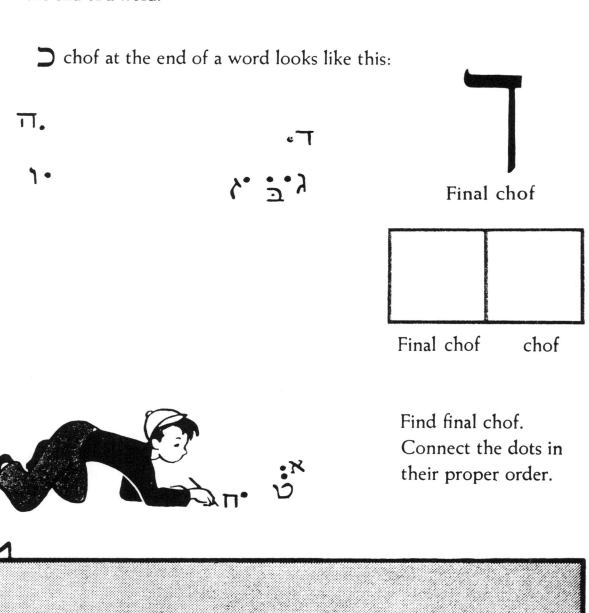

Final chof

Final chof   chof

Find final chof. Connect the dots in their proper order.

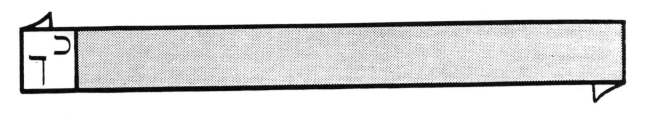

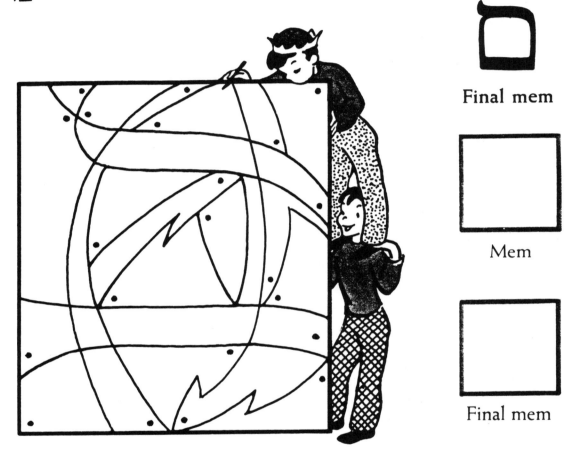

מ mem at the end of a word looks like this:

Final mem

Mem

Final mem

Color only spaces that have dots and you will find final mem.

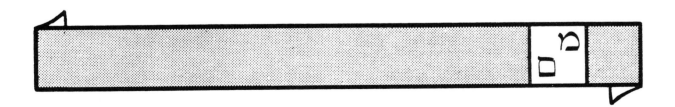

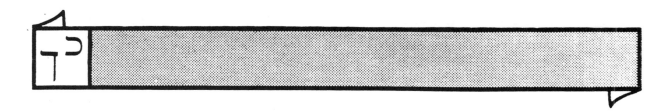

כ ד

ב nun at the end of a word looks like this:

ן

Final nun

Nun

Final nun

Color this final nun.

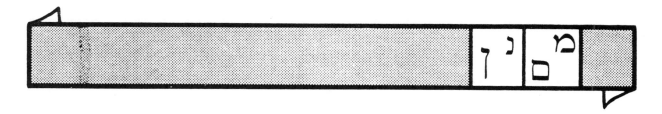

מ ם נ ן

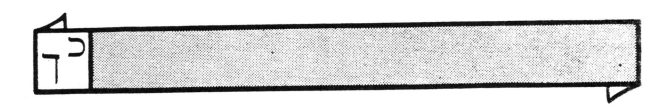

כ Fai at the end of a word looks like this:

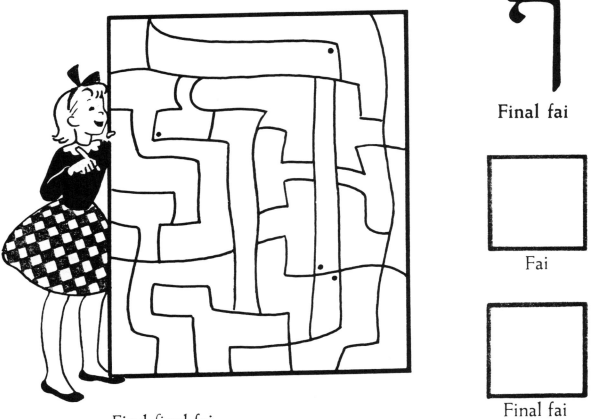

ך

Final fai

Fai

Final fai

Find final fai

Color the spaces that have dots.

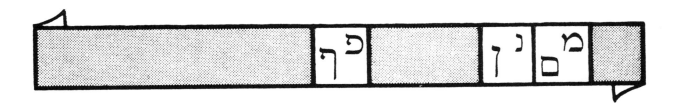

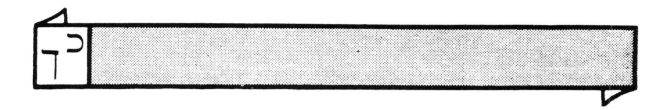

צ Tsadi at the end of a word looks like this:

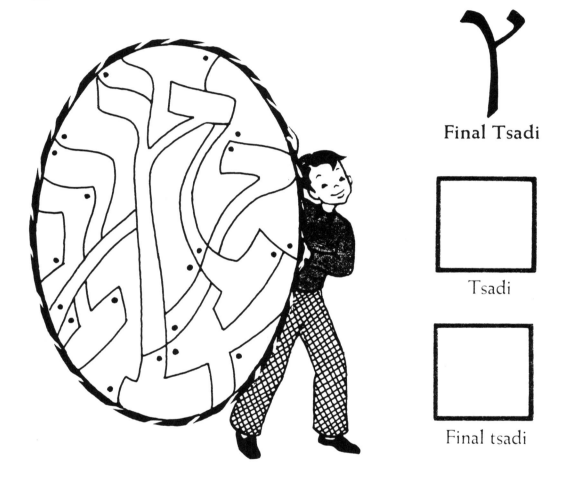

Final Tsadi

Tsadi

Final tsadi

Color all spaces that have dots and you will find final tsadi.

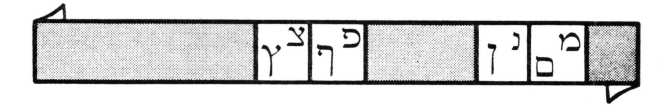

Color chof and final chof red.
Color mem and final mem blue.
Color nun and final nun green..
Color fai and final fai orange.
Color tsadi and final tsadi yellow.

Draw a line from the letters to their final letters.

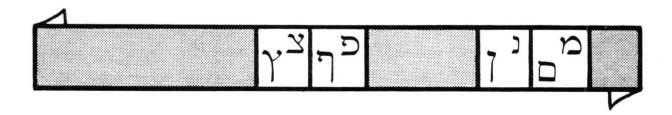

THE MIXED UP LETTERS

ת	ט	שׁ	מ	ה	ק
ל	ר	ו	ע	נ	בּ
פ	ן	בּ	א	ס	ד
ם	י	כּ	תּ	ז	צ
ף	ד	ע	ח	שׁ	גּ
				כ	פּ

These letters are all mixed up. Print them where they belong on the next page. As you finish each box on this page, color it in lightly.

THE RIGHT ORDER

hai	dalet	gimel	vet	bet	alef
kof	yud	tet	chet	zayin	vov
nun	final mem	mem	lamed	final chof	chof
final fai	fai	pai	ayin	samech	final nun
sin	shin	resh	koof	final tsadi	tsadi
				tov	tov

Print the letters from the previous page in the correct boxes.

ALEF BET PARTY GAMES

WHAT'S NEXT?

The first child calls out any letter in the Alef Bet. The second child must give the letter that follows it. If he is correct, he may call out any letter he wishes and the next player must give the letter following that one. If a player makes a mistake, he drops out of the game and the next child gives the correct answer. The last player in the game wins.

I OPENED MY HEBREW BOOK

First player says, "I opened my Hebrew book and there I saw a _____ (mentions a letter of the Alef Bet)." Next player repeats and adds the following letter. Each player repeats what the others said and adds the next letter. When Tov, the last letter of the alphabet, is reached the next player can continue with Alef. Any player who forgets a letter or makes an error is out. Last player left is winner. (Use only the 22 basic letters of the Alef Bet. Don't bother with finals and undotted letters.)

THE MISSING LETTER

This game is good for 2 to 4 players.
Take a good look at the circle.
Try to remember where the letters are placed.
Players close their eyes while the leader hides one letter
      with a button or coin (penny or dime).
Leader says, "Open eyes!"
First child to name the missing letter is the next leader.

This is how we write the letters of the Alef Bet in script.
Write each letter in the space next to it.

פ	כ	א
ך	כ	ב
צ	ד	ב
ץ	ל	ג
ק	מ	ד
ר	ם	ה
ש	נ	ו
ש	ן	ז
ת	ס	ח
ת	ע	ט
	פ	י

Can you write your name in Hebrew?

_____

MORE ALEF BET GAMES

Alef Bet Telephone

Children are seated in a circle. The first player whispers three letters of the Alef Bet, in any order he wishes, to his neighbor who whispers what he heard to his neighbor who whispers to his neighbor. Whisper as fast as you can and don't change the message. The last player stands up and tells the group what he has heard. This is fun!

Party Partners

Here is a good way to choose partners. Use drawing paper, one sheet for each couple. Write a letter of the Alef Bet on each sheet and cut in half, jig-saw fashion. Place on half in one pile, the other half in another pile. Divide the group in half. Let the members of the first half choose a piece from the first pile and the members of the second half from the second pile. Then they try to match halves. Those with matching pieces hold up their letters and become partners.

Name It First

Divide the group into two teams, each facing the other. The leader holds up a card wit ha letter of the Alef Bet on it, or pints to a letter on an Alef Bet wall chart. The first players on each team compete to see which one call out the name of the letter first and scores a point for his team. Then the leader holds up another card and the second players compete, etc. right down the line. The team with the most points, of course, wins.

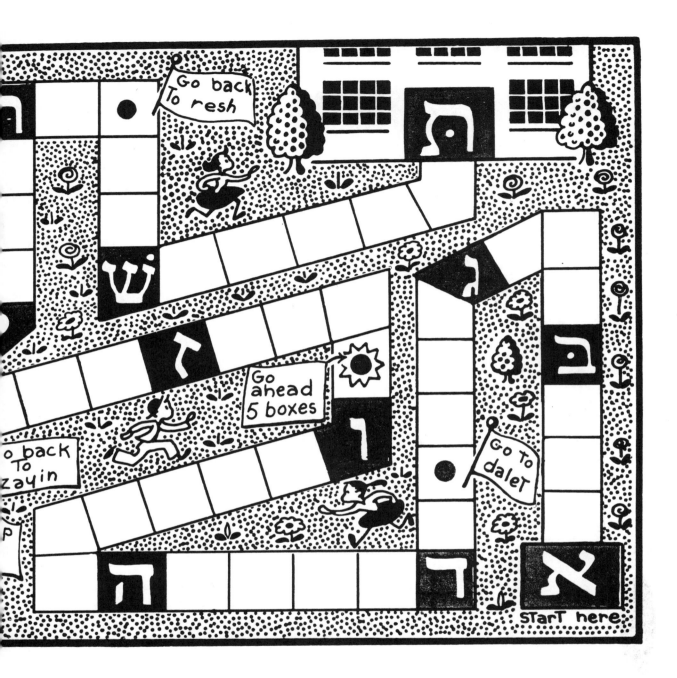

ALEF BET RACE

Two, three or four children can play this game.

Each child has a button for a marker.

The one who reaches ת first wins.

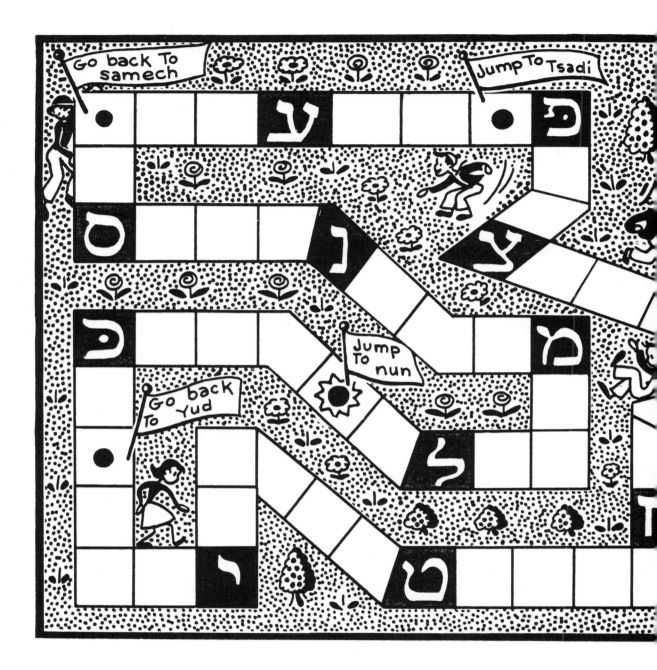

RULES : Flip a coin to move. Each player in turn flips the coin once and makes the move.

Heads — Go ahead 2.

Tails — Go ahead 1.

Black box — Go back 1.

Black dot —
do as indicated.